SEASON'S GREETINGS
FROM
GEORGE

Selected works by
George Mackay Brown

Short Stories

A Calendar of Love (1967)
A Time to Keep (1969)
Hawkfall (1974)
The Sun's Net (1976)
Andrina and Other Stories (1983)
The Masked Fisherman and Other Stories (1989)
The Sea-King's Daughter (1991)
Winter Tales (1995)
The Island of the Women and Other Stories (1998)

Novels

Greenvoe (1972)
Magnus (1973)
Time in a Red Coat (1984)
The Golden Bird: Two Orkney Stories (1987)
Vinland (1992)
Beside the Ocean of Time (1994)

Season's Greetings from George

The Christmas Cards of George Mackay Brown

G

Galileo Publishers, Cambridge

Published by Galileo Publishers
16 Woodlands Road, Great Shelford, Cambridge, UK, CB22 5LW
www.galileopublishing.co.uk

USA: SCB Distributors
15608 S. New Century Drive, Gardena, CA 90248-2129 | USA

Australia: Peribo Pty Ltd
58 Beaumont Rd, Mount Kuring-Gai, 2080 NSW | Australia

ISBN: 9781915530073

The Publishers thank Ingirid Morrison for
her permission to reproduce these cards and to Simon Fraser
for permission to reproduce his illustrations.

FOREWORD by INGIRID MORRISON

Ingirid is George's niece and the owner of the collection of cards which form the basis of this volume.

When we arrived home in 1982 from working and living for eleven years in Africa and started receiving Uncle George's cards, we were thrilled at receiving a new Christmas poem each year. We were even more delighted when one year he collaborated with our nephew Martin Brown, who made a lino-cut image, and George wrote a simple poem to match the illustration. George continued these collaborations, but with the artist Simon Fraser, at which point the cards became more and more elaborate.

Before 1982 George contributed to some cards with Gerry Meyer, his friend and editor of the local newspaper, *The Orcadian*, who along with his wife Nora, had a special card made each year. Their daughter Elizabeth was an artist and their cards used her picture alongside a poem from George. My parents kept some of these cards which are now in my possession.

I have never disposed of a hand-made card and have a lovely collection of special cards, but none so special as those contained in this book. Do enjoy and take delight in both the words and the beautiful art.

Ingirid Morrison, Stromness, April 2023

INTRODUCTION by WILLIAM S. PETERSON

For many years in his Orkney newspaper columns, George Mackay Brown commented in satirical tones about the modern custom of sending out Christmas cards. Nearly every December he described to his readers the difficulties of compiling lists of names to whom they must go, the awkwardness of writing a brief inscription on each card, and the fatigue associated with this annual routine. Yet we should certainly not take this seasonal grumbling at face value. We must remind ourselves that Christmas cards, like many other customs associated with the celebration of the birth of Christ, had changed dramatically during Brown's lifetime. In a later article published in the *Tablet* (19/26 December 1987) for example, he recalled that 'Christmas cards were just beginning when I was young. A family might receive a half-dozen or so; they were rather ugly, more like funeral cards, than greetings. They were set in a solemn row along the mantelpiece, among the tea-caddies and the china dogs.' We should also bear in mind that Brown had been raised in a Presbyterian world conspicuously unenthusiastic about Christmas as a religious holiday, though later, as a Roman Catholic convert, he became increasingly sensitive to the symbolic Christian overtones associated with the year's final month.

There is also evidence that decades before he tried to create his own Christmas cards, Brown was collaborating with the photographer William S. Thompson (then located in Fort William but formerly of Kirkwall) in the production of seasonal greeting cards: an advertisement in the *Orkney Herald* (6 December 1949) offered cards by Thompson with photographs of 'St Magnus Cathedral, Deerness Links, Rackwick, Hoy, Finstown and Stenness Loch. Each card carries verses by George M. Brown, Stromness.' (It is not clear whether any of the Thompson cards have survived.)

In the 1960s his brief Christmas poems were usually written for cards commissioned by Gerry Meyer, editor of the *Orcadian*, and his wife Nora (a few of them are reproduced on the following pages); but by the early 1980s Brown was creating his own cards, and they of course reflected even more accurately his deep responses to the yule season. One important theme that emerges is Brown's unwillingness to relegate the story of Christ's birth to a distant land and remote century. He emphasises instead the strong presence of the mysterious infant in modern landscapes – often a dark, cold Orkney setting. Increasingly in his Christmas poems he seems to envision the Palestine of the Gospels as a foreshadowing of Brown's own world of bleak midwinter Orkney.

The cards created by Brown for his personal use frequently displayed a text inscribed by Robert C. Robertson, a calligrapher commissioned by the bookseller Renée Simm. And many of the illustrations were created by Simon Fraser, an artist who was a friend of Brown's nephew Erlend Brown and was living in the village of West Linton, southwest of Edinburgh. Finally, I should add that for some years after Brown's death, his friend and executor Brian Murray carried on the tradition by sending out Christmas cards with previously unpublished poems by George Mackay Brown, three of which are reprinted below.

THE CARDS

With Best Wishes

for

A Merry Christmas

and

A Happy New Year

from

Mr. and Mrs. Gerald G. A. Meyer

44 Dundas Street,
Stromness,
Orkney Isles.   Christmas, 1954

CHRISTMAS

O little desert town,
    How silent are your streets
Now night comes down!

From a tavern here and there
    Only a ribald song
Steals on the air.

The Roman in a strange land
    Broods, wearily leaning
His spear in the sand.

The inn-keeper by the fire
    Counting his gold, hears not
The cry from his byre;

But rummaging in his till
    Grumbles at the joyful shepherds
Dancing on the hill;

And wonders, pale and grudging,
    If the queer pair below
Will pay their lodging.

GEORGE MACKAY BROWN.

With Best Wishes

for

A Merry Christmas

and

A Happy New Year

from

Mr. & Mrs. Gerald G. A. Meyer

44 Dundas Street,
Stromness,
Orkney Isles

Christmas, 1953

They come to a town, moon-dappled. It snows, and grows
                                                    dark . . .
    The folk yawn through their prayers, and go to bed.
The crystal hill rings with a sheepdog's bark.
    Under the inn one candle is burning red.

This is the town. But where is the fated prince?
    What pillow holds his sweet miraculous head
In this poor street of hovels and furtive sins?
    Under the inn one candle is burning red.

The crimson star meanders through the sky
    And stands, a throbbing index, over the pub
        Where soldiers rattle dice on the sodden bar.
    The strangers descend, and find the sharny crib.
Dazed with light, they hear like a child's cry
    The candle speak to the milennial star.

GEORGE MACKAY BROWN.

St. Magnus Cathedral, Kirkwall

Winter strips the shivering world
  And the solstice darkens on.
Now the leaves are torn and hurled
  Underneath a famished sun.

Still our island kirk abides,
  And the branches' classic dress
Shows us what false summer hides—
  Saint Magnus in full loveliness.

—GEORGE M. BROWN

With Best Wishes

for A Merry Christmas

and

A Happy New Year

From Mr. & Mrs. Gerald G. A. Meyer

44 Dundas Street,
Stromness, Orkney Isles   Christmas, 1952

OLD MAN OF HOY

You do not follow prophecy or star,
Stone king,
But make a single gesture at the west,
Atlantic and sunset, far
From the seasonal dances of god and
      plant and beast
And man approaching the station of
      Last Fire.
Teach us endurance, Lear,
That after the time of stone and flames
      we yet may sing
Gloria round the miracle in the byre.

GEORGE MACKAY BROWN.

Season's G

from e
Nora
&

Springbank,
Stromness,
Orkney.

tings

hristmas, 1966.

The Three Kings

They're looking for what, the three kings
Beyond their border ?
A new Kingdom, peace and truth and love,
Justice and order.

One was black and one was brown
And one was yellow.
A star crooked its jewelled finger.
The three kings follow.

How did they fare, the three kings ?
Where did they dine ?
They lived on a crust or two
And sour wine.

One was yellow and one was black
And one was brown.
They passed a scorched and rutted plain
And a broken town.

Whom did they meet, the three kings
Among the thorns ?
Herod's captains hunting
With dogs and horns.

One was brown and one was yellow
And one was black.
Here's what they found, a refugee bairn
Wrapped in a sack.

What did they do, the three kings
When they got home ?
In Vietnam, Rhodesia, Kashmir, troubled they bide
Till the Kingdom come.

GEORGE MACKAY BROWN

Greetings from *George*

6 Well Park, Stromness, Orkney

Acknowledgements

The following co-operated in this student project :
George Mackay Brown of Orkney composed the poem.
David McClure, DA, ARSA, RSW, executed the illustration.
Messrs Valentine & Sons Ltd kindly permitted their
apprentices to carry out the colour separation in their works.
Platemaking and printing by apprentices in the
Department of Printing.
Ivorex board by Messrs Tullis Russell, Fife

Christmas Poem

WE are folded all
In a green fable
And we fare
From early
Plough-and-daffodil sun
Through a revel
Of wind-tossed oats and barley,
Past sickle and flail
To harvest home,
The circles of bread and ale
At the long table.
It is told, the story,
We and earth and sun and corn are one.

Now kings and shepherds have come.
A wintered hovel
Hides a glory
Whiter than snowflake or silver or star.

George Mackay Brown.

DANCE OF THE MONTHS

January comes with his ice-crown.
February spilling thaw and snowdrops.
March, bursting loud cheeks!
Then April, with a troop of lambs and daffodils.
May, keeper of peat-hill and cuithe-stream.
June, covering the night fire in the north.
July, tall and blue as lupins.
August with the cut cornstalks.
September, dusting cobwebs from the lamp.
October, good witch, with apples and nuts.
November, host to shades and hallows.
December with snowflake and star.

In the inn of December, a fire,
A loaf, a bottle of wine.
Travellers, rich and poor, are on the roads.

George Mackay Brown

to Ingrid & Charles & the girls
from George

Christmas 82

Robert C. Robertson scripsit

24

HOUSE OF WINTER

At last, the house of winter. Find
On the sill
Intricate ice jewellery, a snowflake.

Open one dark door. Flame-flung,
A golden moth! Soon
A candle flame, tranquil and tall.

It is a bitter house. On the step
Birds starve.
In the cellar, the poor have only
            words to warm them.

Inside one chamber, see
A bare thorn.
Wait. A bud breaks. It is a white rose.

We think, in the heart of the house
A table is set
With a wine jar and broken bread.

George Mackay Brown
1983

Happy Christmas!

To
Charles & Ingrid
and the girls

From
George

To
Jacbue & Maria
from
george

Christmas 1984

Robert C. Robertson scripsit

FISHERMEN IN WINTER

Such sudden storm and drifts
    We could see nothing, the boat
        Fluttering in a net
        Of reefs and crags.

The islands, blind whales
    Blundered about us. We heard
        The surge and plunge
        And the whining, all around.

Farm women had set stone lamps
    In the ledges that night.
        The village lamplighter,
        He had not thrown

Over the village his glimmering net.
    The skipper glimpsed one star
        ~Soon quenched~
        But it beckoned to

A poor island with one croft.
    We beached FULMAR. We took
        Up to the croft door
        Two fish from the basket.

George Mackay Brown

✦ LAMP ✦

The lamp is needful in Spring, still,
Though the jar of daffodils
Outsplendours lamplight and hearthflames.

In summer, only near midnight
Is match struck to wick.
A moth, maybe, troubles the rag of flame.

Harvest. The lamp in the window
Summons the scythe-men.
A school-book lies on the sill, two yellow
    halves.

In December the lamp's a jewel,
The hearth ingots and incense.
A cold star travels across the pane.

✦ GMB ✦

Christmas Greetings
from
George Mackay Brown

Make merry then, poem
With bronze sonorous vowels, with
splashings of light
on a winter page

CHRISTMAS POEM

from
George

Few bells in Orkney now, and only a
                    candle here and there
To announce, joyfully, Christmas:

Not in Hoy of the purple hills
Or in the Isle-of-the-Kirk
Or in Mainland with its fertile coat
                    of colours
Or in Ninian's isle
Or in the isle of the pilgrim earl and the
                    little queen with
                    hushed cold folded
                    hands
Or in Eynhallow, busy once
With bellboy and bringer of flame to
                    the beeswax

Martin Brown

A boy draws with scissors
a star, a fish, a flower
from the winter whiteness

George Mackay Brown

Happy Christmas to all
Love,
george

THE WINTER HOU

We never gave a thought to housebreakers
In our Orkney childhood.
Doors, summer and winter, were innocent of keys.

'Oh', cried our elders
Out of the depths of *The News of the World*,
'What vagabonds in the south
Breaking into people's houses at night and thieving!'...

But that only happened in big rich houses
– Masked shadows
Stuffing silver and gold plate into sacks, in cities,
While the rich people
Laughed, danced, drank wine and made merry below.

We had our own housebreaker, and
We wrote letters to him,
Ardent sooty lum-borne letters, *Dear Santa*...

A happy Christmas
and a good
1991

Love
from
George

36

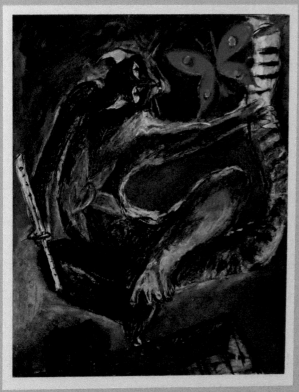

Sarah & Simon Fraser Illustration from Letters to Gypsy (Balmain Books 1990)

We found
An apple, a picture-book, and a sixpence, on Christmas morning.

George Mackay Brown

DESERT ROSE

No one will sing your beauty, the poet said —
You must live and die alone.

Three travellers out of the morning rode.
They lingered. They stirred my incense. They journeyed on.

No shower or shade —
I suffered all day the barren gold of the sun.

A star lifted its head
And seemed to murmur to me alone.

All beyond time are made,
Star and poem, cornstalk and stone.

Now to the House-of-Bread
I guide three hungry gold-burdened men.

Midnight, rejoicing, shed
Dew in my cup like wine.

ERT ROSE

your beauty, the
        poet said —
d die alone.

t of the
morning rode.
stirred my
ey journeyed on.

—
the barren
of the sun.

A star lifted its head
And seemed to murmur to me alone.

All beyond time are made,
Star and poem, cornstalk and
                        stone.

Now to the House-of-Bread
I guide three hungry gold-burdened
                        men.

Midnight, rejoicing, shed
Dew in my cup like wine.

George Mackay Brown

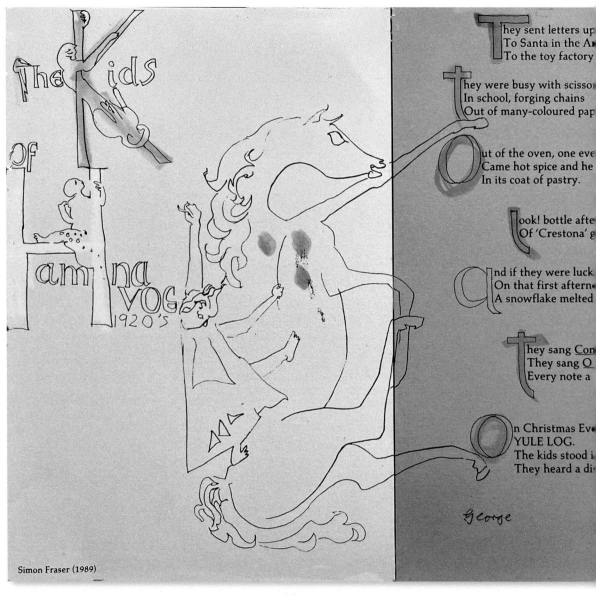

The Kids of Lamina Voe
1920's

Simon Fraser (1989)

They sent letters up
To Santa in the A...
To the toy factory

They were busy with scisso...
In school, forging chains
Out of many-coloured pap...

Out of the oven, one eve...
Came hot spice and he...
In its coat of pastry.

Look! bottle afte...
Of 'Crestona' g...

And if they were luck...
On that first aftern...
A snowflake melted

They sang Con...
They sang O...
Every note a

On Christmas Ev...
YULE LOG.
The kids stood i...
They heard a di...

George

40

The Kids of Hamnavoe

They sent letters up the lum, flaming
To Santa in the Arctic Circle.
To the toy factory there.

They were busy with scissors and paste-pot
In school, forging chains
Out of the many-coloured paper.

Out of the oven, one evening
Came hot spice and heaviness — the black bun
In its coat of pastry.

    Look! bottle after bottle
    Of 'Crestona' ginger wine, quickly ageing.

And if they were lucky
On that first afternoon free of school
A snowflake melted on their noses.

    They sang *Come All Ye Faithful*
    They sang *O Little Town of Bethlehem* —
    Every note a shivering star.

On Christmas Eve someone called from the street
    YULE LOG.
The kids stood in dark doorways.
They heard a distant shouting from Graham Place.

(1989)

41

A Calendar of Kings

They endured a season
Of ice and silver swans.

    Delicately the horses
    Grazed among snowdrops.

        They traded for fish. Wind
        fell upon crested waters.

            Along their track
            Daffodils lit a thousand tapers.

    They slept among dews.
    A dawn lark broke their dream.

For them soon
The chalice of the sun spilled over.

    Their star was lost.
    They rode between burnished hills.

A fiddle at a fair
Compelled the feet of harvesters.

        A glim on the darkling road.
        The star! It was their star.

In a sea village
Children brought a

    They lingere
    By the carve

A midwinter inn —
Here they unload t

Sarah & Simon Fraser

e horses.

f the dead.

es.

George Mackay Brown

George

A Calendar of Kings

They endured a season
Of ice and silver swans.

    Delicately the horses
    Grazed among snowdrops.

        They traded for fish. Wind
        fell upon crested waters.

           Along their track
           Daffodils lit a thousand tapers.

    They slept among dews.
    A dawn lark broke their dream.

For them soon
The chalice of the sun spilled over.

    Their star was lost
    They rode between burnished hills.

A fiddle at a fair
Compelled the feet of harvesters.

        A glim on the darkling road.
        The star! It was their star.

In a sea village
Children brought apples to the horses.

    They lingered
    By the carved stones of the dead.

A midwinter inn –
Here they unload the treasures.

WYE WINTER

Equinox to Hallowmas, darkness
    falls like the leaves. The
      tree of the sun is stark.

On the loom of winter, shadows
    gather in a web; then the
      shuttle of St Lucy makes a pause;
      a dark weave fills the loom.

The blackness is solid as a
    stone that locks a tomb.
    No star shines there.

Then begins the true ceremony of
    the sun, when the one
    last fleeting solstice flame
    is caught up by a midnight candle.

Children sing under a street lamp,
    their voices like leaves of light.

George Mackay Brown

*from
George*

Simon Fraser

CHRISTMAS

'Toll requiem' said sun to earth
As the grass got thin.
The star-wheel went, all nails and thorns
Over mill and kirk and inn.

The old sun died. The widowed earth
Tolled a black bell.
'Our King will return', said root to bone,
To the skeleton tree on the hill.

At midnight, an ox and an ass
Between lantern and star
Cried Gloria... Lux in tenebris...
In a wintered byre.

from
George

George Mackay Brown

Simon Fraser

A snowflake
Came like a white butterfly on his nose.

His mother's bucket
Was blue splashings at the well.

And grandpa
Was notching books like stars on his lines
Down at the noust.

The school locked for Yule
—Time was a bird with white wings.

A swan on the loch
Bent its head like a flower.

He was lost on the hill till sundown
In a dream of snow.

Hunger and lamplight
Led the wanderer home.

A black peat, stirred
Unsheathed claws like a cat
On the purring hearth.

One white star
Walked slow across the pane.

George Mackay Brown

WINTER: An Island Boy

Simon Fraser

A snowflake
Came like a white butterfly on his nose.

His mother's bucket
Was blue splashings at the well.

And grandpa
Was notching books like stars on his lines
Down at the noust.

The school locked for Yule
—Time was a bird with white wings.

A swan on the loch
Bent its head like a flower.

He was lost on the hill till sundown
In a dream of snow.

Hunger and lamplight
Led the wanderer home.

A black peat, stirred
Unsheathed claws like a cat
On the purring hearth.

One white star
Walked slow across the pane.

George Mackay Brown

Publisher's note:

There were in fact four versions of Simon Fraser's illustrations for Winter: An Island Boy, but we have included just two of them in this volume.

Publisher's note:

This was the last card that George sent before he died in April 1996. After his death, his literary executor, Brian Murray, continued sending cards with George's poems and we end this book with three of these, on pages 54-61.

Otherwise this volume is limited to the cards George himself sent in his lifetime and which are in the collection of Ingirid Morrison.

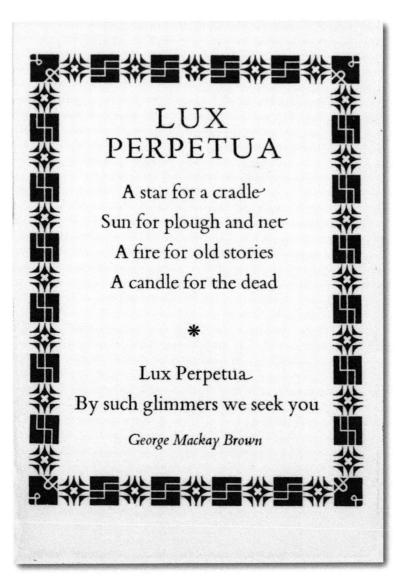

LUX
PERPETUA

A star for a cradle
Sun for plough and net
A fire for old stories
A candle for the dead

*

Lux Perpetua
By such glimmers we seek you

George Mackay Brown

The Fisherman's Word

I put the whisky bottle to my mouth
And pass it on.
We drink in a ring of salt and silence.
We were on the beach before dawn,
We drove down the *Orfeo* without a word.
Nothing all morning; barren circles, the bars of the sea unbroken.
At the ebb's turn
The wind shifted about from west to south.
And the answering sea unlocked his hoard
And a dozen boats
Pulled in shocks of herring like corn.
And the fish-fraught waters still brimmed on and on
Between the islands
Till our hull was spangled with scales and our ribs were sore.
The fisherman's word has been spoken.
We flush salt throats
With the danger, boredom, plenitude of a day.

The ploughmen sing round the fire, we stand at the door
Watching the silence.

George Mackay Brown
March 1965

First Publication
Christmas 2005

54

The Fisherman's Word

I put the whisky bottle to my mouth
And pass it on.
We drink in a ring of salt and silence.
We were on the beach before dawn,
We drove down the Orfeo without a word.
Nothing all morning; barren circles, the bars of the sea unbroken.
At the ebb's turn
The wind shifted about from west to south.
And the answering sea unlocked his hoard
And a dozen boats
Pulled in shocks of herring like corn.
And the fish-fraught waters still brimmed on and on
Between the islands
Till our hull was spangled with scales and our ribs were sore.
The fisherman's word had been spoken.
We flush salt throats
With the danger, boredom, plenitude of a day.

The ploughmen sing round the fire, we stand at the door
Watching the silence.

George Mackay Brown

March 1965

First publication
Christmas 2005

A Christmas Shower
-A poem sequence-

Farm Children

Up at the Bu farm
Seven shirts white as snow
 Were spread on "the horse"
With shadows-of-flame on them.
Seven children
Were lost in white sleep,
 Apples of sleep on their faces,
Outside, the white hill.
 In a fleeting kindle of sunset.

Quarry

Tinkers sit at a driftwood fire
 In the lee side of the quarry.
'the Laird's house
 Came out of this quarry'...
'the free Kirk too'...
'they carted stones from here
 For Simon the merchants shop'...
 Snowflakes, gray moths
 Drift about the fire'.
They rig molasses drums and a patched sail
Between them and the stars.

The Empty Hall

The Hall is shuttered and locked,
 The twelve fires are out.
 The Laird and lady
Won't be home for Yule this year.
 The three hounds are in kennel.
It's very dark and cold in the Hall tonight.
The windows of sixteen crofts
 Flush with fire and lamps.

Yule Brunnies

Twelve sun-cakes
    Lie on the hearth of Biggins,
        One for each month.
In the morning
    The small bright cakes will lie on a plate
        On the table.
June, September, March   the year
    Is eaten by solemn mouths
Plough and scythe
Lie in the dark byre.

Stars and fish

The sky shoal is out tonight,
Stars in a surge!
Two fish on a small plate
suffice
For one croft table, for the everlasting
    World hunger

Solstice

How shall we know
The Sun
Won't grow weater and frailer
Till he's a dead king
With hair frail as snowflakes
And a star locked in his eye?

In the croft kitchen
A child sleeps
Through a night of storm and star gifts.

Hawkers

I walked on the white road

And I met three hawkers
One after the other, with packs.
The Hawkers
Raised hands in greeting, all three.
    I walked on in deep snow to the Ale-house

Christmas Party

Where are the young ones going?
They are going
Past the lighted croft windows
To the fiddles and guitars
    In the community centre'
Lights cut the night like scissors
The boy from the big farm
    Is coming to the dance in his new car.

"No Whiskey bottles"

    Cries Tom the doorman - Bouncer

George Mackay Brown
Winter 1987

First Publication
Christmas 2016

BEST WISHES

PENELOPE

"No more. The last voyage. The deep chair,
A book, your spittoon and the fire.
    Forty sea years, you've been home
    But a few sandfalls of time....

"I don't mind if you go to the pub
Twice a week, with Bill or Rob.
    A gray man now, I think
    You're by with fighting in drink....

"No harm at all in caulking the boat
In winter, and pushing her out
    In May, and rowing alone
    Under the crag, with creel or line....

"Peat-bank, tattie patch. The hill
Is a green wave always still.
    All drown there, in time, and fare
    To the God-acre at the shore....

"The sight of you on the track,
Sea-chest hoisted, leaving or coming back
    -No deeper pang in life,
Whether of joy or grief....

"All's over now. Pull in your chair
Closer, old seaman, to the fire,
    Mansie the cat on the rug,
    A fleece of ale in your mug"....

"Such word-storms! It's dawn, and I'm still up
Setting a whittled gale-blown ship
    In an old rum bottle - Mag drifted deep
    In the doldrums of sleep."

George Mackay Brown   First publication
September 1986   December 2009